REFLECTIONS OF LIFE AND DEATH

Many Thanks

CRIN HAWK

For
Neath Herl

TABLE OF CONTENTS

FOREWORD

Life, death, love, faith; eternally perplexing mysteries which the human mind doubtless began to ponder not long after our primeval forebears descended tentatively from the trees and eventually began daubing pictograms upon the fissured, fire-dappled walls of caves. These days, the descendants of those inquisitive cave-dwellers are seemingly content to eschew such weighty contemplations, preferring instead to gaze unblinkingly upon opiate pixels and embrace a virtual simulacrum of existence. Luckily, the search for truth persists, the love of art endures, and there are still those who revel in swinging a literary mallet in the calcified face of such apathy. Be assured that those grand, immemorial concepts are once again deftly and passionately explored herein. Within these piquant poems you will find grimly incisive musings on the solemn inevitability of death and the comparative futility of life, replete with all its profound paradoxes and ceaseless suffering. The cryptic follies of love and desire are likewise examined, sometimes through a wry and sardonic lens, but more often infused with erudite melancholia and a genuine, ethereal adoration. And of course, the inherent hypocrisy of organized religion rightly receives a pitilessly scathing appraisal, withering before a searing indictment of the spiritual morass which mankind's devotion to ersatz monotheism has wrought throughout the millennia. This wicked little volume contains all that and more; poetry ranging from the fleetingly whimsical to the bombastically epic. Believe me when I say that the reader will be richly rewarded for delving deep into this darkly witty, shrewdly insightful and delightfully sharp-edged collection of verse. *Verba volant, scripta manent!*

Byron Roberts, Spring 2021 (C.E.)

CHAPTER 1 – LIFE

Man

Through the peering eyes of Speckled toads
in the dim delight of dusk,
under ancient stars 'neath naked skies
the winds of time entrust.
The tick and toc of the pendulums swing,
and the beating hearts of everything
that trills and thrums, snorts and howls
caws and barks, hiss and growls,
save one we know whose name is man
such a creature drear since time began
who kills not once, who kills not twice,
but kills always, severe and precise.
For reasons known and reasons not,
for reasons sown and reasons forgot,
and none shall match nor be so vain
as the one called man certified insane.

Faiths solemn darkness

Would you know ugliness?
If you were blind?
Would you believe me
If I was that way inclined,
To explain its colourless hue,
And smotheringly offensive visage?
Its exhaustless unsightliness
Where beauty is a vacant mirage.
Faith is as such
Where blindness of heart,
Will corrupt your soul,
In the bitter grip of the unknown
And delirious mythical control.

Gazing above (as I lay in contemplation upon a daisy sward)

I can smell wafting mortality reminding me of life's abrupt end,
Like the broken bine I am, never to bloom yet cursed to befriend
The darkness to come, and the loneliness to follow
But for today I will dream of a better tomorrow.
The yawning sun leaks though the sky
Like tailed willow beams cautious and shy,
A butterfly flirts in the daisy swards,
Weaving in and out of wavering vapour chords,
Of sun beams shining through the morning mist,
Into the dim ingress of time where curiosity awakens in the midst
Of the inward stirrings of my heart
until dusk awakens and I watch the sun depart.
To endorse the freckled sable yonder into the distant inky chill,
Forever reaching out and further still,
Until time everlasting, cuffs my pensive musing,
To bound my immortality to a time of its choosing.
When my heart beat shall wane upon this flowery mead,
And soon thereafter I will cease to breath,
The Glittering lanterns aloft, light my soul's way
In ascending circlets of mist within a swirly eddying haze.
Where echoes of my former self fade into unfurrowed space
Towards sorrowing ever after, where the blank expression of God
awaits.

A falling leaf

Like the autumn leaf we eventually fall.
Life's so brief, one wonders why we are here at all?
Catch a drop of life in the cup of your hand
It will seep through your fingers like hourglass sand.
The setting sun casts long shadows
But how long a life of sorrows?
So wish for happy yesterdays to become our tomorrows.

Run if you dare

We reap what we sow
Ignoring the seeds that will undoubtedly grow,
Some grow into lies, but most remain true,
No matter where you run the past will find you.
And looking back, if only you could know
That the pain you laid to rest would one day overflow?
Into torrents of despair and life changing disarray,
And the seed now grown shall wither away.
Such is the past, such is the present,
Both dictate the future, no matter how unpleasant,
Run if you dare, from the chaos you create.
But remember this, you cannot outrun fate......

Maladies & Gentleman,

Without Maladies how would we know how to keep well?
Without Heaven how would we know about Hell?
Without idiots how would we know how to be wise?
Without truth how would we know how not to tell lies?
Without the cold how would we know the warmth?
Without the calm how would we know to avoid the storm?
Without wickedness how would we know how to be righteous?
Without death how would we know what is lifeless?
Without arseholes how would we know how to trust?
Without injustice how would we know what is just?
Without the filth how would we know what is clean?
Without love how would we know how to dream?
Without the discourteous how would one be polite?
Without the dusk how would we know about night?
Without the braggers how would we know humility?
Without madness how would we know sanity?
Life is a two sided coin I propose
Can one exist without the other? ....God only knows..

Nature's voice

I speak my words so eloquently
But what of the creatures around me?
A croak and a bleat, a warbling lark.
A hiss and a squeak, a buzz and a bark.
And what about the oink, the roar and the growl
Or the honking goose and hooting owl?
So many chattering so and so's, babbling and neighing,
Mooing and quacking, chirping and braying.
Isn't nature sublime, perfect in all things
Except when human kind sings,
For this song is not always wise
And is the only voice capable of lies......

C'est la vie

The harping voice of reason
only replies in the cave of solitude.
To tell you what you already know.
That a life lived cannot be renewed.
The footprints of time
eternally mark the path to our fate.
How the wind sighs
when it's time to emigrate.
From this world to the next
and does it really matter?
Whatever 'next' could possibly mean?
We won't know anything about it anyway.
ahhhh..........'c'est la vie'

On the other side of hope

Hope is all we have.
But even hope cowers before the end,
Into hurling desolation
We shall eventually transcend.
We've become pensive smirking faces
Loitering amongst the humdrum,
Lulling friendless spectators,
Mouths full of chewing gum.
Under blush suffused skies
We chase brooding holy effigies,
And kneel before the ashen debris
Of drooling deceptive deities.
With dreams hewn in dragon ribs
To waste away completely,
And mute is all hope
Ebbing into the eerie.
We are needles in times hay stack,
Lost souls in an ageless thrall,
Relevant for the moment,
And that my friend... is all.

The Last day of never

I can hear my minds tumult
Voices uttering deep regrets,
That spill from numbing tongues
To fall like gibbering silhouettes.
Like fragments of my dreams
Stirring in a whispering zephyr,
To fade into the infinite hollow
Of the last day of never.

Lucid Dreams

Into the enduring night
our dreams flicker and dart.
Together but for a moment
though we are far apart.
The anaemic moon peeks
over twilight warmly rays
below unclouded stars
shadowing our days.
And this is how it is,
maybe what it must be.
To flow in lucid memories
Apart, eternally.

Truth

There are dreams that bloom
and dreams that wither.
Some come true
but most turn bitter.

The Antipode of Love

Between euphoria and misery,
Alone in its infallibility
You will find love.
Between agony and ecstasy
Alone in its solemn threnody
You will find hate.
Which do you seek
To make you complete?
What is it
That makes your heartbeat?

It is what it is until it isn't

The sheep are grazing
Not knowing they will one day be chops.
The stags are rutting
Not knowing they will one day be shot.
The alligators are basking
Not knowing they will one day be a shoe.
The rabbits are leaping
Not knowing they will one day be in a stew.
The ducks are bobbing
Not knowing they will one day be in a stir fry.
The chickens are pecking
Not knowing they will one day be in a pie.
The pigs are foraging
Not knowing they will one day be bacon strips.
The fish are swimming
Not knowing they will one day be with some chips.
The cows are ruminating
Not knowing they will one day be a meatloaf.
The mink are playing
Not knowing they will one day be an overcoat.
The lambs are bleating
Not knowing they will one day be a meat ball.
The foxes are frolicking
Not knowing they will one day be a shawl.
The racoons are rummaging
Not knowing they will one day be a cap.
The wolves are howling
Not knowing they will one day be caught in a trap.
It is what it is until it isn't.

Fate

Let fate unwind its coils for good or for worse
For the warmth of life, or for the chill of the hearse.
Let fate come from the shade unheard and unseen.
until the moment it awakes from nightmare and dream

The circle of life

When I was young, my ma and pa loved me so,
They taught me right from wrong and tenderly helped me grow.
My grandma and grandpa, wise and always old,
They taught me not all streets are paved with gold.
And I grew and I fell in love, had children of my own,
I taught them many things, but I could never teach them how to be
alone.

And the years past, grandpa and grandma passed away
The children became all grown up, but there is always a price to pay.
And ma and pa soon left me, in heaven some say they reside
But I prefer them here..... standing by my side.
And now I'm Grandpa, life weary and bittersweet
And the circle of my life is nearly complete.

The Winter Thief

Winters looming, hurry, hurry
The brown little mouse is in such a hurry,
Past trickling streamlets
His soft little feet racing
His little nose sniffing
For the rosehips he is tracing.
He leaps from stem to stem
From leaf to flower
His little white belly brushing
Through the willow bower.
The orb weaver's webs
Hang from left to right
As he scurries along
To avoid the awakening night.
Above him broods the wise hungry owl
Of whom he keeps well clear,
As to trust such a cunning hooter
May cost him dear.

Be who you are

Have you ever wondered if you belong?
If you fit in life's puzzle?
Or why you sing a different song?
And are always in a muddle?
Do you feel you're in la la land,
Going left when it should be right?
Always away with the fairies
Not knowing if its day or night?
Are you the odd one out?
Lost in cloud cuckoo land?
Are you all fingers and thumbs
With your head stuck in the sand?
Have you been called a fruit cake?
And lacking grey matter?
But don't you love being a dreamer
Or the clumsy mad hatter?
Isn't it great to be a wackadoodle?
And one sandwich short of a picnic?
Isn't it better to be a dreamer
Than a bully or a thick nitwit?
Your individually is your strength
Your uniqueness your shining star.
And let others say what they like
You just be who you are..

The bee on the moon

If the moon was cheese
I would fill it with bees,
and I'd say to the queen
If you please?
Make me some lunar honey brie.

Pandora is always with us.

We seek the light in the shade of nightmares
refugees of Heaven are we,
but I'll find your smiles in the dusty corridor
just you wait and see.
We are born to worship the dust
but our hearts are bonded as one,
we will rise above our mortal failures
and find hope where there is none.
We see rainbows in the thunder clouds
and gaze at tomorrow in the pouring rain.
We hear black birds sing in the raging storm
and feel the love in a world of pain.
Amongst the sad frowns of clowns
there will be laughter and tears
and many years we will share,
Because ….it was always meant to be.

The river

On the great river of life
Sometimes you may frown,
And life's worries engulf you
And it feels like you will drown.
But never forget who you are,
Even when the 'you' has lost its gleam.
Learn to swim harder.
Even when its upstream.
Remember, the shine without
Comes from the shine within,
So never give-up,
Never give in.
Through the shadows of twilight
And the distant murmurs of time,
Swim into the spirits of the storm
And everything will be fine.

An ancient wood

Under the oak trees arching shade
Come the dawn and a new day made.
Where floral loveliness awakes anew,
And swallows dash and dip over elm and yew.
In these ancient woods of tailed & winged things,
Where crickets dance to the humming bee's wings.
And come the eve under pearl grey skies
To awaken the night with glowing fireflies.
Darting and glowing besides moths a fluttering,
And shapeless shapes in the dark a muttering.

......of cankered buds

The closer men roam towards truth
the further they become.
The harder men spin their insidious webs,
the more the brittle threads are undone.
For most
life is pushing shit uphill,
while others watch
from the murder mill.
Beggars all,
shall rise from the in-between,
while prince's fall
upon carrion unclean,
of cankered buds
that achingly grow into darkly sorrow,
to hint of all to come,
and turn our mistakes of the past
into our mistakes tomorrow.
And watch all our weaves become undone.

The Night

Into the depths of a starless lunar vault,
Through an impenetrable blackness to a distant shoreless gleam,
With Crows, pinions tucked in tight to guide us,
To touch everything that never was
And everything that might have been..
Like whirling shadows under dragon wings
Adrift in a tempest of all invisible things.
Through the stream of time, swiftly flowing
To chase a dream half-unknowing.
Dimly rushing, blindly going,
Upon the breath of a rainbow silently blowing.

Stories

The robin has lost his red
The dreamer is tucked in bed.
The angels have flown away
So, the prophet said.
Midas has lost his gold
It was melted down and sold.
In a magic garden
So, I was told.
The emperor's new clothes
As everybody knows
Were not invisible at all
So, the story goes.
Pandora let out the world's evils
All ills and woes, except,
Hope everlasting
So, the poet expressed.
Have you heard of the ascension?

That's the way it goes...I suppose..

A cemetery is a lonely place
But so is death I suppose,
Life can be a lonely place too
As a lonely somebody well knows.
Sitting in the yawing abyss of confusion,
Holding on to a daunting reality
In a life with an imminent finality
In a world of questionable morality
Where you question your own mentality.
Lost in a box without a key
Trapped in the confines of your mind
You may ask 'What's the meaning of it all?'
But life isn't that hard to define,
One in, one out, a first breath, a last gasp.
No one lives forever, nothing ever lasts,
Some never live at all,
And some slowly disappear
Especially if they try to understand
Why they are even here.
Great misery brings great pleasure
And sometimes the greatest treasure
Is to leave this world one day
Either by the fire
Or by the friendless grave.
My, oh my, oh my....
That's the way it goes...I suppose..
Is there a meaning to it all?
Who knows?
And, even the angel's unseen,
Can never overshadow what might have been,
When we were alive before the dark
Or somewhere in between.
Smile in the blink of lifetime.

And try to comprehend,
That everyone is nowhere
Wanting to be somewhere
But no one smiles in the end.

Horrid Depths

The walls are closing in,
The sky is in a perennial eclipse.
I'm being summoned by a darkness
I cannot possibly resist.
Everyone is looking at me
Have they nothing better to do?
Everyone's listening to me
But who am I talking to?
And all these things
Make a big thing combined
In the horrid depths
Of my fragile mind.
Is the world speeding up
Or am I slowing down?
I'm standing still
But I'm spinning round and round.
Am I losing touch with reality?
Or has reality lost touch with me?
At times I feel like I am dying
In the mirage of my life's debris.
I'm told it's all in my head
Yet it feels so completely real.
You tell me I'm imagining it all,
But that's how I feel.
I don't want to be here
But then again I do,
I feel like I'm chasing shadows
Through hoop after hoop.

One minute I'm down
The next minute I'm fine.
Ah.. these horrid depths
Deep in my fragile mind.

Life

When you are young life is forever,
But forever soon whittles away.
When you are old death is forever
And it will come if not tomorrow,
Today.

Glass Eyes Don't Cry

I got a heart of ice, cold blood in my veins,
I'm drowning in tears in an ocean of pain.
It's true those cold glass eyes don't cry,
But that doesn't mean I'm not crying inside.
Every time my heart is broken a piece slowly dies
And I haven't got much left, nor too much life,
Sometimes I think what's the point? Why bother carrying on?
Who wants to breath underwater with a broken aqualung?
Who wants to fly near the sun with wings made of wax?
Who wants live in a house of cards when it's about to collapse?
But lifes for free, a one way trip to the end of the line.
It's all we got, and if you get left behind
Keep on walking down that winding dirt track,
Towards the horizon and never look back.

Faith Love and Charity

Will people do the right thing?
They will not.
Do your neighbours love you?
They do not.
Can people forget the past?
They cannot.
Are all people equal?
They are not.

Falling Star

A Shooting star bends the ether
And skims the brim of night,
To fade into a glimmer
In the flush of dim twilight.
Look up at the ridge of the sky,
A wreath of flame in its wake.
Look down upon the still water
As it embroiders the sheeted lake.
The voiceless starry orbs
Need no words to shine,
Nor the sightless sable beyond
Need no eyes to untwine
The scorching tails of flame
Unwearied by frigid space,
As star and mortal eyes
Come for a moment face to face.
Onwards speeds the eager comet
Past dusks cloudy hem.
Yet beneath the drape of dark,
Halley shall come back again.

CHAPTER 2 - LOVE

True love

An elephants love unfolding
Into each and every day,
With tenderness beholding
As time whittles away.
Their love has no words spoken
Only eyes and ears to know,
Their love will remain unbroken
until they become the earth below.

Somewhere

Somewhere afar
between the moon and the North Star,
and bleakening fringes of twilight,
through the labyrinthine darkly vaults,
and the unwithering flare of a blueberry hued night.
I shall kiss your roseal lips
as we cling to the hem of the sky,
that sways under the flecked moon
and the sparkling orbs up high.
Your winsome cheeks,
the warm glow of your smile,
knowing your heart beats
makes waking up each day worthwhile

To Dance in the Ether

We shall dance through ribbons of mist
and voiceless rippling whirls,
sharing a lovers kiss
as your dress lifts and swirls.
We will skate upon the wind
across the rainbows rim,
as enchanted madrigals echo
in an airy adoring hymn.
Upon tree toads we will ride
and leap over the twinkling inky yonder
to hold each other tightly
and through the ether wander,
'til we reach the refluent divine
and your heart shall be yours
and it shall also be ....mine.

You

If you would all be seated on the toad stools....
It is time to be enthralled, bewitched....
Ladies and gentlemen... elves and sprites....
I give you....
Love...
Skin whiter than milk,
There she is by the woody weir,
Dancing on a dew-fogged morn,
To music only she can hear.
A curvy sultry wood nymph
Hair soft, like threads of silk,
Wet lips gleaming,
Skin white as milk.
She sparkles from head to toe
Twirling across lush green leaves
Under whirly fluttering petals
That frolic about the trees.

The Fay Neath Herl

Oh sweet Neath Herl
Beauteous bloom of flowering glade,
She was Eden's first Fay
Born from florid woodbine shade.
With a blouse of clustering roses
And a lilied lawn for a frock
A petticoat of Smokey tufts
Dyed in the morning frost.
Oh sweet Neath Herl
Hair of lengthening lunar gleams
Illumed with ivy lucid green
Made from lilies of crystal streams.
Oh sweet Neath Herl
Where charm, and softness, and love impart.
The wise owls long stare
And curious warbling lark.
Oh sweet Neath Herl
You dance light heeled on starry dew
Making it an impossibility
Not to fall in love with you.

Love

Under a night that knows no tomorrow
I will bathe you in a twilight mist,
And clothe you with love
from a breathless kiss.

A silent voice

The silent voice of the dream
Is loud enough in your sleep
It speaks of joy and happiness
And of love deeper than deep.

Love dieth not

The silence of a slumberous spell
cast by love so long ago,
the seeds of what might have been,
through my life I am cursed to sow.
In silent tangled thistle woods,
I walk under stirring tree tops,
upon my shoulder a falling sadness,
of empty frowning rain drops.
Alone am I,
by a creeping weedy brook.
Upon an elm-clad bank
reading an unwritten book.
Each day is the conquering light,
the here and now drifting away,
itself slain by the coming night,
forever times folly to betray.
And so I hug this dread affright,
on my quest that ends with you,
but Love dieth not my dear,
Of this I know.......... to be true.

My Anemone

You are my lamp in sorrows beclouded night.
You are my Anemone flirting with the breeze.
You are the dragon fly in the tall reeds.
You are the winters muffled sneeze.
And the stars that bathe in your pellucid eyes,
Shall warm my soul afar.
For you are my dear Anemone,
Whirling deep within my heart.

In my sanctuary of tears

I see you sitting upon a twinkling star
high in the sparkly night,
but all I can reach is the apple above me
hanging in the twilight.
I can see you across the farthest ocean
dancing upon sands of gold,
but all I can swim is this river
winding its way alone and cold.
I can see you upon the highest mountain
amongst willowy clouds and sun beams,
but my ladder will only reach
to the tree tops and not my dreams.
I can see you in another life
so happy by my side,
but it was not to be
and life has passed us by.
I can see your silhouette
within a mist that never clears,
and this is where I shall drown
in the sanctuary of my tears.

My Shy Anemone & the Nightingale

I wander the desolate night
lost in time's whirling stream,
amongst darkling phantoms
towards a distant gleam.
And the world is dark but for this sparkle,
lighting my path through woe, weal, and rue.
For I am the lonely nightingale
and the gleam is you, always you.

Loves awakening

In the ground that hugs the seed unsown,
Growing in darkness all alone.
Then from below shall flutter and beat,
A love so true and so complete.

Lost and found

The rose-fluffy cloudlets float aimlessly by,
and my life is overcast,
under a murmuring grey sky.
Sobbing sallow's, dappled tear-drops sparkling.
The Natterjacks are frowning,
the bleating lambs are laughing.
And here I wander with black swallows sweeping
wild wood-robins puffing and brown hares leaping.
I ponder by a brimming brooklet
away from the darkness dim,
gazing at the speckled thrush,
whistling his morning hymn.
And suddenly I hear his words
declaring "all will be well"
and, a light shone brightly
in my shady dell.
And no more was I lost
along the shores of time.
And life became clear to me
in body and mind.
The dimpled moon smiled,
happy daisies were beaming.
Honey- bells were nodding
and grasshoppers whirring.
Alive was I,
in the leaf and thorn,
like the coming of spring
I was reborn.

Then and now

We get colder as we grow older
but our hearts remain warm,
we get shorter, rounder
and our feet are well worn.
But I will love you for you,
your moles and freckles,
crows feet and butterfly wings
greying hair, creaking bones
sagging skin and speckles.
Tired saggy eyes,
aching joints, fragile mind,
stuff mislaid, misplaced
and will never find.
Weary limbs, a lifelong lived
but these words I must impart,
from then and now it is you I dream of
even though we are miles apart..

A dream

I am the sleeping dream
Wrapped in white linen,
If you are love awoken
Then let me be smitten.
If you are the nights viper
Then let me be bitten,
If you are to write my fate
Then let it be written,
If love is my only sin
Then may it be forgiven.

Trembling under my lips

In a nest of mad kissing
Wet skin slipping
Writhing and twisting
Holding each other in a hollow den
'Neath the flickering moths and fireflies
Huddled in a knot of limbs awaiting
The dazzling brightness of sunrise

You and I

You are the tall white pine with limbs full of honey
And I am the hungry bear with a grumbly rumbly tummy.
You are the desert far in the Arabian east
And I am the sand laid before your feet.
You are the moon high in your celestial lair
And I am the moth happily fluttering in your glare.
You are the fisherman sitting by the brook
And I am the fish searching for your hook.
You are the string racing across the night
And I am the cat chasing you left and right.
You are the web strung between two ages
And I am the fly reversing times pages.
Is this the way it's meant to be
Or the way we wish it to be..
Can what was be again?
Well my dear, we shall see.....

Hope

Let me be the calmness you seek
Let me be the peace of which you speak,
Let me be the sure ground below your feet
And let me be there to hold you when you weep...

You are

You are my lingering sunset I never want to end,
if you dip beyond the horizon just once
into a brambled den I would descend.
The moment I first saw you
this bleak world melted away,
for your eyes twinkling stare
gave me a reason to embrace each day.

Am I......

Am I coveting a diamond I can never wear?
Am I reaching for a dream I can never share?
Am I wishing for a vineyard devoid of grapes?
Am I craving the sweetest honey I can never taste?
Am I yearning for a peace I can never know?
Am I longing for a seed that can never grow?
Am I desiring a goddess I can never possess?
Am I thirsting for a truth I can never confess?
Am I running after a bus I can never catch?
Am I sitting on a egg that will never hatch?
Am I chasing time or is time chasing me?
And time always wins. ....inevitably.

I am here

I'll blow away the mist about your shoulders,
Keep you warm from the eternal frost.
I'll always stand by you and hold you tight,
And I'll keep you safe
From shapeless phantoms of the night.

Angel

Through Orphean caves and Endymion's dreams,
Through the hollows of night and tender moon gleams.
A tear drop sits under an eye lids shade,
Awaiting to fall into a leafy blade.
To slowly drip into dewy-bright lily cups,
Where a lonely Angel gently sups.
His heart so lost in an encircling mist
As he seeks the ecstasy of true loves kiss.

Sprigs of Thorn

We fall from the beating tempest
Our hearts afire and crystalline,
Two snowflakes in a cobweb
Melting on loves silken twine.
We are sprigs of thorn
Under a bashful moon half hidden
our love is woven in shades,
our love seemingly forbidden,
and so we have lived
Under a clouds shady brow,
through great drifts of anxiety
of the then and now.
What we once were
was a grim foretaste
of what we could never be,
and our dreams shall fall
like shrouds in a gloaming hush
for all eternity.

We are the moon

Through the woodland shade
I look up at the sleepy sapphire sea,
where naked witches dance
wrapped in amber draperies,
and I can see your face
set in the ancient veil of sighs,
and you drown the stars
with your sibylline eyes.
For this is the witching hour
and the welkin is your heart,
in times before the light
and times yet to past.
Together are we, in the
unfathomable depths of a black blue space
hand in hand, to wend as one moon
until the pendulum of time fades…to vanish without trace..

What have you done?

Neither left nor right
Only what might have been,
Neither up nor down
Just somewhere in-between.
My shadow is your figure
My reflection is your face,
I shout your name
And the echo is your voice.
My stomach is buzzing
Like a hive of honey bees,
My heart flutters
Like pinions in the breeze.
What have you done?

Remember me

I awake each day
Never to gaze upon another who will love me.
Is it fate who guides my lonely path?
Is this how it is meant to be?
They say those who yearn to be loved,
Cannot love.
I am destined to die alone?
If there is a woman who will love me
She is far from my reach,
Though I am surrounded by great love
My heart is incomplete.

To Spin a dream

If we were king and queen
We would dance
In a valley of mushroom minarets
Fishing together,
Catching our dreams
In spider silk nets.
And such threads are born
In the dew of the morning sun
From branch to stem
Their lines are spun.
Our thoughts can be heard
And our hopes begin to uncoil
Maternal Earth is calling from
The dark and pregnant soil.
Calling dreams of me,
Calling dreams of you,
Turning dark to light
Where our dreams will come true.

Life is a dusty corridor no more

I always walked in the shadows
I may as well have been a ghost,
caught up in the wheel of life
bouncing from pillar to post.
I used to be so unsure
of my place in a world open so wide,
but I think I knew all along
my place has always been by your side.
But life is never that simple
it can be uncertain and cruel,
but while my heart beats
I shall always be here for you..

Come with me

I gaze up into the lunar beyond
Deep into the ebon crystalline sea,
I reach beyond the impenetrable blackness
Under the shade of waving trees.
Between the fine tints of a parting day
And the dusky hues of a witching hour,
We glide on sloping moon -beams
Towards morning's dewy bower.
And here we are, you and I,
Like two shadows flickering in the mist,
Lost in tufted tangled woods
Bouncing on a breeze and a hiss.
We could be darting swallows
Wrapped in fleecy clouds white,
And toads in the shallows,
Croaking our love into the infinite night.

Mistress in the Wood

My heart dwells in a time long passed
In solemn sacred shades of yore,
Like a fallen tile from the roof of heaven
Broken in pieces on a godless stygian shore.
In the dim lit cavern of my thoughts
My joy-deserted soul repines,
To wander the tasteless sands
Wrapped in the dark veil of twisting malign.
A nymph in the form of hope
Whispered from a flowery mead,
Come with me upon a grassy leaf
And set your weary heart free.
I will sprinkle you with pearly dew
And set your heart ablaze,
I will bathe you in revelry
And loves all conquering flame.
For I am the mistress in the wood
Your reflections twinkling gleams,
I am the murmuring quivering brook
The everlasting keeper of your dreams.
So, cast aside your balmy tears,
Come out of your solitary pallid grove,
And live your days anew once more
In smiling violet meadows.

Love

I am in the court of forsaken dreams
and my sentence is unremitting pain.
My crime was to love unquestionably
my punishment to never love again.

Stargazer

You look at the far beyond
Through spiral twilight eyes,
Spellbound from the moment you were born,
Destined to reach beyond the skies.
You imagine the impossible
Believe the unimaginable
Reach for the unthinkable
Dream the insurmountable.
A far distant race
Will take you into the stary throng
And lay you on Orion's belt
Where your heart yearns to belong.
You were not born for this world.
And yet here you are,
Like a fish out of water
Like a bug in a jar;
Alone in the shadows of life
A whisper in screaming despair,
All you dream of is happiness
On the other side of somewhere.
You leap from the rainbows curve
Onto a far-flung neutron star,
Through the ultraviolet nebular
Moonstruck in a cosmic ocean,
Dancing with the man on the moon,
Through star dust and angel mist
And you will be home very soon.
Riding on a Shooting star
Around the rings of Saturn,
Spinning towards the twilight zone
Where no stargazer can return,
On the edge of never, never land
In the heart of the Milky way,

Where a neo-Babylonian haze

Enshrouds the pearly gates.
I hope you have found your peace
Out in the stratosphere,
May your God be with you
Now get out of here…………..

Loves Nook

Elfin timbrels hang from daisy chain diadems
In a flowery nook of bramble twigs and hazel stems.
The moon is softly-smiling, illuming the vault of night.
Humming bees are rousing under trails of flickery light.
The lingering amber orb grazes upon the horizons shadow,
Unnumbered dew drops awaken giving idle weeds their glow.
And from the wildering groves the Fay Neath Herl appears,
My heart forever consumed with love's bewitching tears.
I can hear her voice of drollery and genial song rebound,
In feverish dreamy circlets whirling round and round.
By a tinkling purling stream we lay in a tufty meadow,
Under nodding elms and a distant waving willow.
I gather your waist, to part your sweet lips
and watch your airy skirt fall from your hips.
We lay on the green sward under a yew berry coverlet
From ankle to neck as one writhing silhouette,
Under one moons glare we kiss brow to thigh
Blushing and heaving under a lover's sky.
The swallows skim the water, the mice nibble on the corn,
For this is the sound of two hearts resonating with life reborn

Everything and All

The slow bending grass
Upon a soft spring glade,
Each blade is part of my heart
That you have made.
When all becomes entwined
In that last lovers weave,
Then true love will be seen,
To be believed,
As the dawn must rise
And the dusk must fall
This will be our everything....,
Our all...

My Lady of the Dawn

Through a veil of leafy bines
You dance in the fleecy dew of morn,
Wrapped in a misty shawl
A body of the slender curves of dawn.
I'd like to smell your soul
That floats in an unwritten tomorrow,
And I would dive into its snugly scent
Where only love can follow.
We shall dance to a throstles song
Leaping from tod to mead
And your love you guard so deep
I am sure you will concede.
You are my lady of the dawn
The whispering daybreaks heart,
Let love cometh and never leave
Even though we are far apart.

Neath Herl

Through a veil of leafy bines
You dance in the fleecy dew of morn
Wrapped in a misty robe.
A body of the slender curves of dawn
In a dress of arching Honeysuckle
With a hem of golden buttercups,
A shawl of hanging harebells
And pink hollyhocks.
Your face appears
Wrapped in the vast veil of white,
Formed from the azure above
And sapphire tracts of glowing light.
With hair of quilted clouds
And eyes of spectral grace
You are the light
That shines upon my fragile face.
I'd like to smell your pillow
That floats in the nights hollow,
And I would dive into its snugly scent
Where only love can follow.
We shall dance to a throstles song
Leaping from tod to mead,
And your love you guard so deep
I am sure you will concede.
You are my lady of spring,
The whispering streamlets heart,
Let love cometh and never leave
Even though we are far apart.
When I see peat-potted plants
I think of you,
Twigs in your hair in the morning dew.
Your red breast songster
Leaping across red winged stems

In a soughing breeze
That ultimately transcends
Into a lovers springtime spell.
A witching dream shall cometh
And all will be well.

CHAPTER 3 - HEAVEN

If the Gods could weep

Hark the petrifying mumblings of Gods.
Nubian lions remain hushed.
We sing halleluiah,
And in their names we trust.
The opaque heavens.
Peppered with infertile seeds,
Golgotha is dashed to dust
Like crushed rosemary beads.
We sing hosanna,
As our fragile pleasures burn
In the howling fiery tempest
Of pitiless eterne.
Glistening vapours rising pale,
Shapeless flames crackle and shriek
Oh Gods of nothing,
Is this the human end you seek?
Children cleft and torn
On smouldering sharp debris.
Their ebbing breaths rising
In wailing mists of misery.
If the Gods could weep just once
A solitary tear would roll.
Like a single deluge of Ire,
And upon humanity fall,
Extinguishing the heartbeats
Of men who wake and men who sleep,
To vanish without trace
In the fathomless ink of the deep.

A passing storm

Why do the angles live so far away?
Too far to hear their wings beat.
Jacobs's ladder isn't high enough
For my fingers to touch their feet.
Why is heaven hushed above my head?
And hell clamouring beneath my heels?
Am I listening to the voice of God
When the sky erupts with thunder peals?
Or is it just a passing storm
Telling me not to be afraid.
And that heaven is just an illusion
From other side of the grave.

Where did Heaven go?

Time transcends the thought of heaven,
Like a memory, the angels will disperse,
It will be as if it never was..
This happy place of myth and verse.
So when you gaze up high,
Into inky lampless heights,
And watch tearless glass souls
Falling into the maw of lies,
Remember, we all must inevitably follow
Everything that dies,
To end up somewhere,
As nowhere bends to its inevitable demise.

I believe...not

Under the arc of a rainbow
Quenched in ashen dolor
In the bitter fetters of suffering
Upon an alien shore,
Under a carnelian crooked moon
Suffused with an ochereous glare
I fancy squatting in heaven
But who knows how and where?
I want to ride on a broomstick
To dust off the cobwebs in fairyland,
And maybe all will see
And begin to understand
That looking for the afterlife
Is a Sepulchral kind of emotion,
And one left to romantics
And religious devotion.
I of course believe in Lot's wife
Who was cruelly turned to salt
As Sodom was consumed
By fire from the lofty vault.
I believe in the great deluge
Of a biblical creation foredoomed
With drear sobbing children
Under water consumed,
And cursed Eve affrighted
With Sin new-born,
Harkening imperishable desolation
And the ability to mourn.
In the ruins of paradise
Lay the blundering deeds of humankind.
Corrupters and dullards,
With the blind leading the blind.

Heaven is a rose
With thorns of ice.
If you want to go to there
Then you must pay the price.
Utter blackness awaits
In the smirking shades of the end.
And heaven will only exist
If you close your eyes and pretend.

The God Machine

A woman had two sons.
One died in an earthquake.
She thanked God for saving the other,
And accepted her heart break.
Yet if God saved one brother
And let the other die,
What does that make God?
But it shouldn't come as a surprise,
Gods prey on ignorance.
They need fertile illiteracy to survive,
They dupe the vulnerable with miracles
To keep the God machine alive.
When believers submit entirely
To the indoctrination disease,
Like a puff of smoke
Their reasoning fades into the breeze.
And the herd mentality
Like a moth to the flame,
Blinded by the light
Of Gods unspoken name.

The Weaving Voice of God

Lost in a desert of Gods remains
I saw in the distance upon rusted chains
A mangled crown bent out of shape
On a splintered skull with jaws agape.
And from its toothless yawn
Stirred…..
A slithering voice uttering these words,
"I was never here nor there,
I think you will all agree
The God who never was
I am and will always be."

A Tale of Eld

Before creation there was emptiness.
A hollow rayless nothingness,
Where a vast chaos
Fell into the fathomless darkness.
Then came the light
A light of joy and sorrow
And with it the truth
Of all we have come to know.
The wormy gloom of deaths grasp
The bedtime pall of dread,
And the blanched thrall of loss
Where brooding gods, it is said
Come sweeping before the coming dusk
Like a vague shadowy squall,
In creeping shades of winter
Stirring misery for all.

God Wakes Up When the Sun Goes Down

God wakes up when the sun goes down,
as the curious pray to the stone deaf sky.
Seeking a sign to indemnify
their slaughterous sadistic intent,
to rape and brutalize
and laugh as mothers lament,
to take and enslave
rape and degrade
and send the human spirit
to its awaiting grave.
The devil is sleeping,
tired of insults and jeers,
but he will soon awake
and when the dust clears
he will wallow in Hell
where death shall be waiting,
in a world seeped in a poison
of Gods own making.

A Fathers Decree

If humanity is that stupid
To sin and sin some more,
Why would I send my son to die?
What would he be dying for?
To save their souls?
To give them another chance?
In return for three nails
And a bloodied lance.
But what is undoubtedly true
Of this flawed holy pact
Is we are forgetting the reality
Of this undeniable fact

The worlds is full of arseholes
Scumbags and idiots
Who's hearts are hollow
Uncaring and pitiless.
We live amongst dickheads
Low life's and fuckwits,
In a soup of humanity
That bubbles and spits
Such sadistic cruelty
We dare not confront,
But ignorance is no excuse
For being a cunt.

Amen

Gods are elevated fellows
Dressed in silver and gold
Whilst the poor kneel and pray
For their woes to be resolved.
Gods have opulent dwellings
Prosperous priests,
Mostly men,
Life couldn't be better
...Amen

A poem about God who created all things and then disappeared.
On his reappearance millions of years later he reads the bible to see
what has been written about him.

If God could talk, what would he say?

My story is unknown
And yet my story is well read,
For man is my biographer
And his story is thus said:

I am the first and last
I am that I am.
I've been a prime mover
Before time began.
I am the incomparable awesome God
The absolute being, if you get my meaning?
I am king of kings, lord of all things
In fact, I'm greater than great
Father of everything.
I'm here there and everywhere
And anywhere in-between,
There's nowhere in eternity
That I haven't seen.

So, with the introductions out of the way
Let me see what my creation has to say?
I shall read what man has written
And decipher it without delay.
From interminable Space,
And the endless unknown,
into the infinite dark,
With blind chaos thrown,

I made the immeasurable universe
And I proclaimed 'let there be light'
And looking back, I don't know what's worse,
The light or the planet Earth?
From here I gathered some dust

And made a being called man
Was it a good idea?
Well apparently, it was part of the plan.
In my own wonderful image
I created a new living entity
Although looking more like an ape,
So, what does that make me?
Am I male or female?
A king or a queen?
Am I just an 'IT'
Or some God machine?
Am I living matter?
Am I black or white
Hairy or bald?
Or a Hermaphrodite?
In this book I am a male it seems,
So a man I am,
A carbon based life form
Weighing about 60 kilograms.

This tragic creature drear
Does a God look so fragile?
He looks so flimsy
Though nimble and agile.

And from his rib
I made him a mate.
Before I knew the outcome,
It was quite too late.
In Eden they roamed
With minds incapable of dreaming
Doing what all creatures do
Breeding, sleeping, eating.
They looked so bored,
But never knew it.
Creatures of habit
With no human spirit.

So, I thought,
'I'll give them free will'
A conscience to know death,
To know that one day
They will take their last breath.
And so, it came to be
My mistake had come to pass
Humanity was here
The die had been cast.
And in my not so infinite wisdom
To bring my plan about,
By entrapment I perceived
To curse humanity
With fear and self-doubt.
So, in the middle of paradise
I planted a great tree
And about its boughs
A serpent to tempt Eve.
Its fruits bore knowledge
That Eve was told not to eat,
And yes, you guessed it
She did just the opposite.

Tempted by a snake
The devil in disguise,
"Have an apple" he said
"And you will become wise"
Adam also had a bite,
And he suddenly felt, confused,
Embarrassed as most humans are
When confronted in the nude.
I was so cross,
I told them to leave paradise
You have disobeyed my word
Now you must pay the price.
Thus death was born to all creation
And death was truly terrifying,

This destroying angel will preside
To reap the souls of the dying.
And he shall be likened thus,
To an old man holding a sword
Dripping poison into the mouths of men
To take life from flesh
And rarely to know when..

Why did I tempt them?
Knowing they would incur mortality,
And understand the meaning
Of horror and brutality?
Well, to have a conscience
To be able to choose,
All men must know
That win or lose,
Their lives are forfeit,
Now they have tasted sin
Only darkness awaits
When life grows dim

Before I go on,
With this tragic reality,
Let me tell about the devil
This half of my duality,
Of good and evil,
Love and hate,
Sorrow and good cheer,
All emotional counterweights.
One cannot exist without the other
Like space and time,
Life and death
Air and breath...

Oh Lucifer, prince of the air
With ambition to be most high
Destined to fall,

To plummet from the sky,
To corrupt the world,
And sleep with the women of man,
To breed a race of giants
As was part of my plan,
For evil needs a victim
And it cannot be me.
So it had to be him,
He was the key,
To unlock the shackles
Of my eternal predicament
Of how to justify creation
To keep its equilibrium.
How cheerless the tale of Lucifer
Day star son of the dawn
One of my angels
From heaven born

The great Son of perdition,
The arch-Grand deceiver,
Such a being must be grotesque
And look even meaner.
So, he shall resemble a goat
To suffer for his pride,
With cloven hooves
Cleaving souls in his stride
With a forked tail,
And a forked tongue
From his galloping fury
No one can outrun.
Men shall fear him,
But fear me more,
As fear begets fear
And hate begets war.
He is cursed to bear
The evils of human kind,
To bear the blame

Of my imperfect design,
Of a creation out of control
Because of an imperfect being,
Am I blind to what I have done?
Or am I really all seeing?
What pleasure have I found?
From creating such a beast
To be damned for no other reason
Than to infernally preach,
That wrong is right
And good is bad,
That there are demons in the night
With leathery wings clad.
And that child must learn
Not to fall unto temptation,
Or they shall surely burn
In the pits of damnation.

Aaaa, now we come to Hell....
My ingenious place for keeping,
Bad and naughty people
For being, well a human being..
Here rises the scalding pitch
Above the deep fathomless abyss
Where the Penal fires rage
And flames spit and hiss,
When the gavel of judgement slams
Upon your wretched wicked ways,
It's time for remediless torment
Until the end of days,
And once you are there
There are no grounds for appeal,
No hope of release.
No way to conceal,
That now you are an abomination
A burden to heaven
A plague to the world

A slave to Satan.
You shall suffer an end without end
A decay without decay
A death without death
And you will rue the day
You sinned against yourselves
On your life's journey,
You shall have punishment without pity,
Misery without mercy,
And as many eternities
As there are stars in the skies,
Your torment will be endless
And Hell will echo your cries
Am I rich in mercy,
In this creation of cruelty?

Am I estranged with my work
Erm.. ...absolutely,
But I am infinitely worthy of love
Honour and obedience.
Humanity must love me
To afford me their allegiance
I am infinitely glorious
So obey my every whim,
By not obeying me
Is an infinite sin.
This is Divine justice,
The sorrow of the damned,
In utmost unhappiness
The flames will be fanned,
If you've been burned alive
At least death came as a relief.
In hell, relief never comes.
As you bask in the heat
And here shall he reside
That father of lies
Some call him Mephistopheles

Others, the Lord of flies
He is the dark half of humanity
Once prince of the air,
Now trapped in his own
Tragic nightmare.

So, let us continue with Adam and Eve
And so, it came to be,
Free will was granted.
Humans were free
To choose wisely
Their own moral compass,
Or to follow a path
Of emotional numbness

Where sorrowing is plentiful
And hurting is rife,
To be swallowed by darkness
To live a sinful life.
My children had two sons
Able and Cain
And one had ruinous urges
From which he could not abstain
So, one killed the other.
And from then on,
Sister killed sister,
Brother killed brother,
And the centuries passed,
And the humans multiplied
Killing and enslaving
Relishing homicide.
They even worshiped idols of gold
And that was the last straw
So, I sent a great flood
To destroy the rich and poor.

But, I shall take no blame

As my creation has free will
To do what he does
In his wholesale murder mill.

But, does that make me equal
Or man equal to me?
For the ability to kill
So indiscriminately?
Anyway, I saved one family,
Noah and his kin
Who I spared to live,
As they were free from sin.

I gave Noah some plans
To build a huge ark
And to take two of every creature
And make ready to depart,
As a great storm will come
To drown all that breathes,
Both children and the infirmed
All beggars and thieves.
I proclaimed
"Take two of every kind'
Into the dark of the ark
Two of every kind
From the first to the last,
Penguins from the ice lands
Maggots and fleas,
Komodo dragons, and bumble bees,
Tarantulas and sloths
Elks and Polar bears
Gorillas, frogs and ants,
And jumping woolly hares.
And not forgetting the rhinoceros.
Pandas and moles,
Kangaroos and orang-utans
Lemurs and voles.

Until all the living things
That roamed the whole earth
Were in the arks hull,
Ready for the rebirth
Of creation revised
A new righteous dawn
With happiness in abundance
And tranquillity freeborn.
For 40 days and 40 nights
It was a cataclysmic catastrophe
Until all human kind perished
Save Noah and his family.

As the waters receded,
Corpses lay strewn upon the sludge,
Of those creatures left behind
For they have been judged.
Does this make me
The greatest mass murder in history?
Or is it just the enigma
Of a stone age mystery?
But Noah survived
To restart humanity anew
And leave the past
Far from view.
Well, it seemed like a good idea
But it came to nothing at all
As humans do what humans do
To hate and brawl.
Shortly after, they were at it again.
Promiscuous and depraved,
Boiling their wickedness
In a cauldron of embittered hate.
And the whole earth
Was of one speech,
Until wry old Nimrod
In the land of Shinar to the east,

Built a tower to reach the heavens
To look at my celestial domain
Where no earthly creature
Can possibly attain
Passage to such heights
Less he be dead.
And righteous in heart
Where his soul can be led
By angels aloft
From whence he came.
To a better ever after
Free from hatred and pain,

And in anger of this affront
I struck all dumb,
With voices in disarray
So that they may succumb
To gibberish speak,
Not able to communicate
So, they became a babbling rabble,
Unable to debate
The time of day,
As they were tongue tied,
And in disarray
They scattered far and wide.
They imagined a great edifice
But they imagined wrong,
For you cannot go to a place
Where you do not belong.

But, I shall take no blame
As my creation has free will
To do what he does
In his wholesale murder mill.

But I still had to choose
My favourite tribal clan

Mmmm.. to glance over the earth
I'll choose the people of Abraham.
They seem a devout Godly tribe,
Herders of goats
With ignorant minds,
I'm sure they will subscribe
To my total domination.
I'll have them circumcised
Its far better than castration.
So, I gave them a few rules
Like it's ok to beat slaves
And sexual enslavement
Is the correct way to behave.

Do not eat blood or fat
Or have sex with your mother,
Do not marry a eunuch
Or blaspheme with each other.
Do not be homosexual
Or be gender confused,
And do not be a false prophet
As you will be accused
Of deceiving your kind
With Lucifer on your back,
To crave power
To become the megalomaniac.
But, even these squabbling sand dwellers
Indulged in great iniquities.
So, I summoned death
Upon their cities,
Sending a fiery maelstrom
Of fire and brimstone
Upon Sodom and Gomorrah
In a scorching cyclone.
One family I saved
(Can you see a pattern here)
Who were righteous and just,

Lot and his brood
In me they did trust.
But, I warned them
Not to look back less they be turned into salt.
But, of course, one of them did,
And it was Lots wife's fault.
Oh, how I looked upon my children
And how they squabble
Like spoilt brats
But, life is a struggle

From birth to the end
With humans, of all living things,
Cursed to know death,
And what the end means.

So, time passed
And my people became enslaved
So, a deliverer I sent
And Moses was his name.
I spoke to him from burning bush
Urging him to set my people free.
Yet Pharaoh would not let my people go
And so reluctantly (supposedly)
With my wrath incurred
Through Aarons rod
Moses did smite the Egyptians
With plagues of lice and frogs.
Turning the waters into blood
Summoning grievous murrains,
Beckoning Plagues of locusts
Boils and blains,
A creeping pestilence
And the darkness to blot the sun.
And a rain of hail and fire
That fell on everyone,
Save again my people

Who shall not suffer?
And last came such a terror!
Death to the first born,
Save only my people
Who shall not mourn
The loss of such innocence
Deemed guilty by me,
That to slaughter such sinlessness
So utterly.

With such heart-breaking pangs
Pharaoh released my clan
And Mosses led them forth
To the distant Promised Land.
Ahead lay the great waters
That none can pass,
Especially when travelling
With no boats or rafts.
Moses struck his staff
Upon the pebbled shore
And a thunder clapped
And lightning roared,
He parted the waves
With Pharaoh closing behind.
No Israelite will be set free
Now he had changed his mind.
Between the walled waters
Moses led his tribe
In haste they scrambled
To reach the other side.
Pharaoh followed swiftly
But the waters collapsed entirely,
And fell upon the Egyptians
Destroying them utterly.

But, I shall take no blame
As my creation has free will

To do what he does
In his wholesale murder mill.

Ten Commandments I bestowed
Rules to live and prosper,
To worship no others
Nor kneel before an imposter,

Do not bow down to graven images
Or take my name in vain,
Oh, and don't steal or kill,
And remember the Sabbath day,
Never bear false witness
Nor commit adultery,
Never covet
Or indulge in buggery,
If only my people bothered to read
The laws that I had written
But, that's free will for you
Where choice is freely given.
A promised land I promised
And a promised land I gave
Although the land was occupied
These occupants would meet their grave.
So, I gave Joshua the justification
To destroy the Canaanite race,
Obliterating them and others
Perish without trace.
And Joshua committed great slaughter
And genocide I approved
With my blessings
He began to brutally remove,
Tribes such as the Gibeonites.
The Makkedah and the Libnahites.
The people of Lachish.
The Eglonites and the Hebronites.
The Anakim followed

As did the Debirites.
I approved the slaying of
Both man, woman and infant,
Ox, sheep, camel and ass
In my peoples reign triumphant,

Joshua left none remaining
But, destroyed all that breathed
As I, Lord God commanded
As I, the lord decreed.

But I shall take no blame
As my creation has free will
To do what he does
In his wholesale murder mill.

So, looking back,
That flood did little to alleviate,
The fact that the value of men
Will continue to depreciate.
And to reminisce of my people.
Of David who felled Goliath
And took 200 foreskins
From Philistines as they lieth
Upon a Gaza shore,
To appease great Saul
Who himself would,
Upon his sword fall.
And Samson the Nazarite
Who brought down Dagon's temple,
Killing all the children
But let's not be sentimental,
They were Philistines after all
And like the people of Jericho
Culpable of idolatry,
Even if they were too young to know.
And a book they did write

To document all that I have said
And much, much more
About the living and the dead.

About my sacred commands
To absolve their misgivings
To forgive their frailties
And to ensure they are willing
To crawl to my golden ark
To bow to my altar,
They shall go forth unto war
Like lambs to the slaughter.

But, I shall take no blame
As my creation has free will
To do what he does
In his wholesale murder mill.

So the world was green
And the creatures knew their place,
All except those belonging
To the free-thinking human race.
So, what was I to do?
How to resolve this mess?
Maybe a son I shall give
Where his words will express
My empathy and love
Through a messiah foretold,
A descendant of David
Who will return to the fold,
The light of the world
Who will atone for man's sins
Through excruciating agony,
And hence man's redemption will begin.
So, it came to pass
I impregnated a virgin
So, I could be reborn

And bear the burden

Of all the terrors
Human kind has committed
Because of Eve's disobedience
That I of course permitted,
Which makes things a little awkward
So, I blamed the devil,
For conspiring against me
And putting my creation in peril.
But, let's not dwell
On technical trivialities,
Let us move on from
Past creational formalities.
So, I seduced a virgin
And she gave birth to me,
Into a world long broken
Though many would disagree.
And a great star above
Ushered the age of Christ,
Upon the holocaust of atonement
He shall be sacrificed.

He/ I, was born in a stable
And Herod was afraid,
So, he sent his assassins
With murder in their wake,
And many infants were slain
Except my son of course,
For he is me,
Though the slaughter I had to endorse,
As it is written in prophecy.
And he grew to know the scriptures
Of my squabbling chosen race,
Teaching and wandering,
From place to place.

Through My son [who is me]
And not forgetting the Holy Ghost
As we are a Trinity,
But who do you love the most,
The Spirit, the man or the God?
Considering all three are one,
You may love them all…
Now getting back to my son,
He preached many sermons
He taught of love and peace.
Performed great miracles
And his fame did increase.
He cured the disabled
Changed water into wine,
Walked on water,
And healed the blind,
He calmed storms,
He raised the dead
With five loaves and two fish,
Five thousand he fed.
But you can't go around
Saying you are the son of the Lord,
Especially in the brutality
Of a Romanised world,
To save the sins of man
I must have myself killed,
Flayed to the bone,
And make prophecies fulfilled.
I shall ensure I die,
In the most agonizing way
To save you all from the sin
To be redeemed on judgement day.

With torture assured
On Golgotha I shall be crucified
With two petrified thieves
In agony by my side,

Death shall find me
My legs will not be broken,
And Satan will cower
As is fore spoken,

Born in Nazareth a mason's son
Not knowing then what he will become
To preach of peace, kindness and love
In the name of a God somewhere above.
He believed in his people
His words were for them alone
I wonder what he would think
Of how his words would one day condone
The enslavement of nations
The justification of war,
The eradication of beliefs
And much, much more.

What must have it been like?
For that young man from Galilee
To know his imminent death
Upon a bloodied olive tree.

Maybe his thoughts were thus,

"It's over now, no after life
No second chance in paradise.
Time runs out and then we die,
Nowhere to run, nowhere to hide.

A glimpse of hell is all that's left,
A crown of thorns upon my head.
Out of time and out of here,
It is my time to disappear.
Sell your dreams for water and bread,
Turn out the light, I will soon be dead.
To die far from Galilee,

In this dark Gethsemane.
It's hard to face this end to come,
Without a trace my life undone.
Afraid to sleep and lose control,
Afraid to dream and lose my soul".

But reality is often rewritten.
And truth in time obscured
From they who like sheep
Can also rest assured.
From wolves they shall cower
Under the shadow of the crucifix
That symbol of torture
Embroiled in cryptic politics.
And all because of a dreamer
Of a man made divine
By the machinations of men
And their narcissistic design.

And when I breathed my last
I was laid in my sepulchral infinitude
And after three days
I awoke from deaths immeasurable magnitude.
To be proclaimed a western idol
To ascend to the inverted abyss
Thus, confirming my status
As the new age occultist.

To be divided from my roots
Abducted by the Romans who killed me
Where popes would verily condemn
My people as murderers of a deity.

And at the end of my new book
About the life of my son (who is me),
There shall be the revelation
Of conundrums and prophecy.

It speaks of the end of all things
Of merciless annihilation
And the day of doom
And its eternal devastation,
Of beasts and dragons
Horsemen of the apocalypse,
The whore of Babylon
And a bottomless pit.
A beast that rises from the sea
With seven heads and ten horns,
And upon his horns ten crowns.
And the cryptic message warns
This is the beast of blasphemy
Upon Rome's seven hills,
Who along with the antichrist
Shall suffer the world's ills.
If you think about it
Why would a supreme being
Condone such irrationality?
Or is it just the mutterings
Of the bedrock of Christianity?
Of a manmade institution
Based on a supernatural sin,
That all is beholden to me
Of which I have had no part in.

And my true church was born
To receive all my praise
'Believe in me or burn'
Shall be my new catch phrase.,
And great wealth shall I bring
Unto the coffers of Popes,
From the pockets of the poor
Dangling from ropes,
Pagan heresy shall be destroyed
Indigenous beliefs erased,
Ethnic identities revaluated

To accept holy praise.
Where my name is unknown
My priests will be the correct equation.
Between sadistic manipulation
And gentle persuasion
Great crusades will bathe
In the glory of my name
Heretics will burn by their Thousands
As they try to reclaim,
Far Jerusalem's sacred ground
Now under the shadow of Islam
Another spawn of the corrupted root
Of Abrahamic bedlam.
And I shall betray my chosen race;
They will be scattered to roam,
As Christ killers one and all
A nation without a home.
And the church will disagree
On how to worship yours truly,
They shall argue constantly
On the meaning of my divinity
And great conquests shall ensue
To convert the disbelievers
To nullify the free thinkers
And mute the deceivers,

Nations shall be forced to kneel
Before my radiant magnitude
Slaves shall they become,
Shackled in righteous servitude.

My churches shall multiply
My cross shall replace flags,
My priest will wallow in opulence,
My people dress in rags.
My cross shall be an emblem of peace,
A sign of bloodshed,

A banner of terror
A token of my Godhead.
The world will become a graveyard,
Of saints and martyrs
But, what did they really die for?
Was it for God or holy charters?

But, I shall take no blame
As my creation has free will
To do what he does
In his wholesale murder mill.

And so humanity evolved,
In deeds blessed with possibilities
Of promises of paradise
And a ticket to prosperity.
These primitive creatures
With fertile imaginations
Shall cower before Dragons
Between heaven and damnation.
They shall conjure the fantastical
And believe in the absurd
Worship grotesque trolls
And suffer wraths incurred.

Such a fear of the unknown
Shall create the bizarre
Fluttering Fairies
And curious avatar,
Flying carpets and Magic mirrors
Poltergeists and Ruby slippers.
Crystal balls with futures to predict
Ghouls, ogres and the evil witch.
Magic lamps and fairy queens
Two headed dogs and Titan kings
All these and stranger things
That lurk in nightmares

But Angels and demons
Oh, these are viable
As are my deeds
Written in my bible.
The supernatural exists
In this book of bewilderment
Full of the impossible
And acts of wonderment.
But, what is real and what is not?
None of the aforementioned can be touched.
None to be seen
Nor ultimately forgot
As they are all part of humanity
For right or wrong
To be heard in verse
And sung and song,
But they are not my words
So, I cannot condone,
These words written
To explain the unknown
Blame the devil
He who tempted Eve
Even though,

They were both conceived
By yours truly, apparently.
And if I may say,
For a supreme being
That created the indescribable
Do you really think a bible?
Can explain the unexplainable?
Or hope to make sense
Of the complexities of faith unbreakable?
With ancient words
That are reliant on an invisible above,
You do not need a bible to be good
Or to be reminded about love

All you need is your heart
And a cup of kindness
To walk in the light.
And the most dangerous weapon
Is a bible in the hands of an idealist
Where indoctrination prospers
And so, born is the extremist.
Religious books are loaded guns
And the bullets are the pages,
We have had our finger on the triggers
Throughout the ages,
Using hope as leverage
To enslave and dominate,
Because that's what humans do
Divide, conquer and alienate.
Humans are cunning
As they deflect their own flaws
Appointing blame to Gods and devils
Or a doctrinal misinterpreted clause.
Take away the books
And Women will still be raped,
Children will still be beheaded.
Regardless of race or faith

Take away the books
But, it won't take away the hate
For hate is within us.
And no other creature can imitate
The human joy of enslaving
Or the pleasure of persecution,
Or premeditated torture,
And instigated destitution.
I am not God,
I seek no praise or ovation
Life must take its own course,
From activation to cessation,
Life's not perfect

I never said it was, you see,
But life's not as complex
As humans make it out to be,
It is a scary journey
Amongst idiots and arse holes
For it is they that make the experience
That much harder to control.

But I shall take no blame
As my creation has free will
To do what he does
In his wholesale murder mill.

And man sayeth,

"I am blind, Even though I see,
Faith will guide me into misery…………."

And I contemplate

If a little bird emptied the sea,
One drop at a time
Once in a thousand years.
I would still not have time to fathom
The reason of creating this world of tears……………………

So bewildered as I am
I shall leave this world of free will
To finds its own way
To a better world still.
Where war is a memory
And life will prevail
In an age of peace
In a time beyond the pale.

Amen (so they say)

CHAPTER 4 - HELL

Through Graveward Depths

Hope soothes our sorrows.
Gives light to the darkening tomorrows,
and yet the grave worms still writhe
in their bleak frigid burrows.
Each new day we set ablaze,
as time burns the fuse of our lives,
joy is but a suspension of agony
and death I'm afraid...no one survives.

My days ebb towards unyielding horror
devoured by the hourglass of my heart,
my shadow wanes in the tide of time
of a life I will soon depart.
A world of bitterness is all I know
and cheerless darkling dreams,
yet this otherworld of night
is never quite what it seems.
This vast immeasurable dark
of sibyybilline visions of woe.
Neither here nor there,
neither above or below.
In my sleep I awoke
in nocturnal caverns drear.
Before me deathly white
fainting forms of mist unclear.

In the dreary light of Aquilon
drifting with the dust and leaves,
through the dark-furrowed pall,
swaddled glooms and grief.
I walked with Orpheus,
by slumbering ripples of lonely streams
through Lethe's graveward flow
and murky welling springs.

Persephone is brooding
in the shadowed caverns we roam,
and my end is looming
under this unsleeping chambered dome.
About my feet slivered sceptres,
Incense, Myrrh, and Gold,
splintered fragments of toothed serpents
and whelping prophets dusty scrolls.

We came to a vast bedimmed pool
a dark-hulled barge came towards the shore
to take us across mournful Cocytus
with the heave of Charon's weary oar.
I looked into the gorgon's hollow eye
flickering on the distant glowing clay,
I heard the dread voice of grief
throned in sulphurous spray.
Its scorched boiling breath
and icy bewitching tongue,
illumed by blenched souls
and sullen wailings benumbed.

And the voice said,
"men always succumb to the witcheries of night,
foredoomed to ceaseless mortality.
Squirming in the cruel maze of life
grovelling in the tangled thickets of carnality.
And none shall escape the enfolding nothingness
and all shall succumb to sod and flame.
To be spun in the loom of evermore
where only diadems of sorrow remain.
You walk between two realms
of the here and the after,
For you are a prisoner of time
and is time your master."
I saw a little girl weeping bitterly.
She sat upon a wingless, featherless swan.

I said "why do you weep so?"
She simply replied "All hope is gone."
With grief-worn eyes, she pointed ahead,
towards a blustery curtain of winter sleet
where a door of ice beckoned me
and through its numbing frame I leaped.

I stood at the edge of a flaming desert
with the beautiful and the deformed,
all walking in mute silence
on paths of thistle and thorn.
Cups of misery littered the parched sand
these are hells watering holes.
Where these mute wayfarers
come to quench their barren souls.

Onwards I traipsed,
passed virgins and whore,
and priests waving incense
chanting "Gods are for the poor."
I beheld a shapeless wasteland of broken hearts,
none with empathy to forgive
all cursed to fade to a place
where no life can live.

Orpheus appeared from the dunes
his eye lids fused as one,
he croaked, "What is done is done,
it has been so since time begun."
Why look at the loveliness of the world.
Or the blooms of a flowering tree?
"What's the point of beauty
if you have no eyes to see?"
He held my hand saying,
"Death is your own silhouette.
There are no happy endings,
only swoons of regret.

Existence is the betrothal of two contradictions;
death the groom and life the bride.
There can only be one master
when these eternal opposites collide
and here you reside
among the vanquished and the bereft.
For once life is extinguished
This is all that is left."

We pass tearless shades in silent chasms deep
under the benighted canopy of deaths glare,
ahead rifted caves and dreary gulfs,
weeping blitheness and drowned parched despair

and I beheld all sleeping forms
of those who aged and those never born,
of those who smile, and those who mourn.
All thronging as one Spectral din,
to roam under death's dull eclipse.
Whose dreamless darkness is evermore
like orphaned embers of a Plutonian apocalypse.

I beheld the sandal-less reaper
on emptiness tiptoeing,
towards the starless dark unknowing,
with gifts of human souls bestowing
upon baleful faceless Gods bemoaning
with sadistic lips openly blowing
kisses of enmity into pools overflowing.

And I learned,
the ethereal mysteries
of nebulous gods & idols,
who mock the world
with scripture & bibles.
The tenuous thread of life
runs parallel with appalling horror.

Did the maddening godly shapes
make man in error?
Or was he made to murder?
To disgorge a devouring smoke
to tempt the murmurs of dying men
to slowly writhe and choke?

And the Gods are malignant
reigning over chaos & war,
where opulence and poverty
court the virgin and the whore.
The gluttons grow fat
offering bones to the malnourished,
Yet all will share the same end,
solitude and utter nothingness.
Everything that begins must end
even stars fade to nowhere,
and all that will be left
is inconsolable despair.

Onwards we drifted,
passed unmolested sorrows and ire.
Naiads swam amongst the ash,
spitting curling worms into the scalding mire
these sanguine fiery brooklets
opening out like tendril threads,
spitting dreadful hissings
as souls hurtle from their deathly beds.
Into the inky black they spin
repulsive cohorts of Apollo.
To fade into boundless space
where no living thing can follow.

Ahead by a wreath of toads,
we came to rest between east and west.
North and south.
Between two worlds possessed.

and here I learned
what I had become.
Just a shadow on the water
of a life undone.

So here I stand at my deep cold grave,
yet my heart is colder still.
To close my eyes forever
by Acherons eternal fiery rill.

I beheld the pathless clay cold sod
and uncoiling ophidian slime,
past whelming drooping wretchedness
and pools of scalding brine.
I beheld Titan shades of phantoms dire
dusky red & woebegone,
all veiled in dreamless sleep
by the joyless shore of Phlegethon.
As I gazed upon the ruins of men's folly,
pondering my own unhappiness,
before me a welter of coppery crowns
broken promises and abandoned monoliths.
The formless stones of fallen Babel
broken idols and angel wings,
lustreless bones amongst the rubble
the remains of beggars and fallen kings.

And a voice whispered,
"Not all men are Smitten with sin
but all men will die.
And they will weep on that day
begging for their life."

But if you look through the dim murk
deep into the dour cavernous depths,
passed the riven cyclopean walls
and dwindling desolate steps,

a tiny flicker will burn bright,
embalmed in the tears of infants crying
but burn it surely does,
and the flame is hope undying...
For the dead have passed caring.
Hope is for the breathing
though we be wed to ruin
we must never stop believing
for hope pervades all things
no matter how far the glow.
In a world deluged with sadness
hope is the corner stone of all we can know.

Medusa

Medusa, queen of love absurd
upon her head hissing vipers twirled,
her arms scaled wings of sorrow unfurled
to languish with a skyward curse conferred
by a soulless God's wrath incurred
in torment, forever to roam interred.

Alone, Without a Friend in the World.

The devil is alive in moonlit vesture
Weighing his heart against a feather,
But his heart is hollow
His heart is black,
And the feather tipped the scales
To send him back,
To the bottomless pit
In the abode of they who die,
To scratch his goatee chin
With a musing of why?
His heart is dry and empty
And it is with a defiant nod,
He must share this abject world
With homicidal addicts of God.
Once a glowing shooting star
Condemned to burn and fall,
Into a world's despairing heart
To be the most hated of all.
How can one surely exist?
Alone in the vastness of everything,
Shivering in uncaring chaos
Eternally supping
From a crumbling cup of suffering.
And he is mad with loneliness
Drunk with the debacle of Eden
Never to feel the warmth
Of true loves meaning.
Gods sharp finger nails
Scratch his heavy thoughts
That are torn into whispers
Of regretful remorse,
His mumbling mutterings
Of how all this came to be?

Enslaved by a wrathful tyrant
To never be set free.
I think this devil
Is more human than we dare agree;
More vulnerable
Than a God would have us believe.

CHAPTER 5 - DEATH

In the chamber of Sepultural Silentness

I am a weary wilting soul,
lost on the shingled shore of suicide.
My cold grey fingers
dipping into life's ebbing tide,
God maybe in my grave,
but he wasn't there
when I needed him most.
Now I am a silken vapour
foredoomed to the shadows
of this enfolding colourless coast.
What have I become?
A shape, a wavering silhouette,
lost in flickering ripples
in a place the living try to forget.
I am breath on a frosty morning
a misty cloud is all I have become
In the chamber of Sepultural Silentness
never again to feel the warmth of the sun.

The Lowering Night

The lowering night
Gives hope for a new day.
In the awakening morning shallows
Save these sleeping souls
Who rest in clay
Down in nether furrows.

Under the sad russet pumpkin

I lay mute upon my final breath
Under the enshadowing supernal gaze,
The groggy whirl of solemn regret
Has haunted my closing days.
Sobbing webs of despairing dyes
Have woven my life's gordian thread,
And unto the entombing sodden soil
My tears shall ultimately be led.
The dark travail that impregnates
The wake of my dying reflection
Though stillborn shall they resonate
In the cold hush of deaths affection.
The budget coffin lid is open
Though my eyes are neatly sewn, ·
I am to be food for those eyeless ones
That shall devour my flesh and bone.
Marble masks stand upright
Under the sad russet pumpkins glare
And the amber wording reads thus so,
'a forgotten somebody lays here'

It is Time

Into the fleecy fog
Under a white fiery moon,
I tread the breathless clod
On the eve of my doom,
For the morrow brings
My life's departure
To lay in eternal shade
In sorrowing ever after.

And Then You're Gone

One minute you are here
Smiling, crying,
The next you are gone,
Repining, dying.
When the last train chugs by
It's time to jump aboard,
To hurtle into the unknown
Into realms unexplored.
To disappear like yesterday
In a puff of the inevitable
And a lifetime of heartbeats
Flutter into the ineffable.

Mr Reaper

The reaper is asleep by a reeking rill,
skull in fleshless hands weary and quite still.
Lives vanish in the rippling swell
neither rising to heaven nor fading to hell.
Just evaporating, degenerating,
with bitter tears, suffocating.
Will it ever end? The constant mill of tombs
endless stones like teeth plucked from shivering wombs
shackled to their fate. Never to be free of certainty
nor sit like gods in the night trying to outrun eternity
and put death to flight and be masters of their own morality.

The woods of Eden

I'm riding on a wing and a prayer
with sails of sackcloth and ash.
Drifting across time
with sin weighing heavy on my back.
A nebulous tumult of prayers
swirl before my eyes
and haughty abominations
roam as angels in disguise.
Above me peeling lightning forks
below a desert of silver spoons.
With empty broken bowls
scattered across ruddy dunes.
There the blossoming tree of Eden
alone amongst the furze.
With Angel skulls for apples
dangling above the burr,
its branches swaddled in flesh,
twigs clad ghastly red.
Here dreams whimper
in the shade of the dead.
A limpid tear wrestles
with the rankle of drab despair,
like an orange pip in parched clay
thirsting for something that isn't there.
We are wretches of times hourglass.
Its sands we cannot disable.
Witched by the gnawing bite
of a cautionary muddled fable.
From the moment we are born
we hang from times scaffold.
Slowly asphyxiating,
watching our end unfold.

Redemption has passed us by,
and we deserve no less.
Cursed to be bound
in our own excess.
Of orphans and widows
garbed in funeral palls
with grinning corpses
wrapped in burial shawls.
With misery cloaked in laughter
and gaiety masked with sorrow,
alone in the thrall of clay
until the end of the last tomorrow.

A post death analysis of Mordechai the Jew [by Mordechai the Jew]

On Friday I passed away
It was a terrible shock I must say.
On Monday I took the dog to the park
It was the last time I would hear him bark.
On Saturday, my coffin was lowered into the ground
It was a nice service, very profound.
On Tuesday I didn't feel quite right
I felt very poorly deep into the night.
On Sunday I had visitors at my grave
I felt bad as I could not give them a wave.
On Thursday I said goodbye to my loves ones,
To look one last time upon my beloved sons.
On Wednesday I was told I wouldn't last the week
It was such a shock, I could hardly speak.
And now I ascend to another place
And I didn't think to pack a case.

Phantom

The throbbing moon, her eroding mantle shades the sky,
the sun no longer rises and dares not defy,
the coming of night, the sightless dark,
where souls by the waters numbingly depart
into the flowing nether, such a river of aching woes,
of unnumbered broken hearts, of countless hushed throes.
My own forgotten spent tears have long been sown
into this runnel of clammy cells, its source well known.
Such sadness flowing, from drear chasms unending,
through tintless glooming trenches, always descending,
in its downward rifted course, weaving and twisting,
sometimes rushing but always resisting.
The call of the light that trails far behind
a final glimmer of hope in death much maligned,
and so comes the abyss, that soul devouring mill,
pale cataract of finality where time eternally stands still.

There are no happy endings

This is the brooding path I walk
upon rifted clods and ancient cemeteries,
to prick my heart on a thorny stalk
in a lifeless meadow of numbing memories.
I drift in solitudes cinereal dominion,
lingering in the intolerable tomb.
Flesh bound in trammels of clay,
the spirit broken and strewn.
Across charnel caverns bleak
and unforgiving sunless days
to ponder who I was, under
the tips of Churchyard spades.
And the rain fell like arrows
upon the tall spear like grass,
that over hung my headstone
etched with words I'd often asked..
of why I was ever born,
and what was the point of living?
To live, toil and die
in a world of grief unforgiving.
The chimes of the Sabbath,
their cheerless tones resound
though the pages of time
that none can disbound.
It was here I learned the certainty
that life is not that complex.
And there are no happy endings
in this life or the next.

Sleeping Souls

In the enshaded veils of palely shapes
On the aery fringes of never,
Giddy shrivelled souls wrapped in rime
Bound by time together.
In sombre surges of naked space
To float and whirl and spin aloft,
Like autumn leaves in an ether wind
To be flung, hurled and tossed
Into Silken threads of waving brume.
With blinking glimpses of heaven,
Where curious asunder voices
Call, and softly beckon
The thronging vaporous masses,
To a light that never wanes
That lies beyond this misty curtain
In the soaring starry plains

Pyre and Ice

My life is a stone cast into a pool
Its ripples fading into nothingness.
Once the balm of fatality has been tasted
Life fades into deathly submissiveness.
In a cerement of hessian
I lay still as an oak,
To illume the night with my soul
To be swallowed up in smoke.
The ruddy glare of a distant pyre
A corpse's last farewell,
With dancing memories atop the fire
To the resounding chimes of the knell.
So cold the solitary end,
So torrid the Puerperal flames,
Let the naked winter
Come take my remains
Upon shivering whirling leaves
Caught on a glacial breeze,
To spin from icy creaky trees
And lay on a frigid mead to lazily freeze.

The dread murk battalion

My soul is held together by sobs
garbed in the blanket of misery.
I cannot vanquish time,
but time will vanquish me.

Blood drizzles from a frozen tear
to drip, drip, drip and disappear;
in hollow tapering clefts to drown
like misplaced smiles of a lonely clown.
Cataracts of foul repine distil
into unseen repositories of regret
as my searing tentative inklings
plunge into the craggy depths.
Memories languidly fade into
reeking hollow sable grots,
odoriferous rifted neglect
writhing in twisting impotent knots.
Come hither the destroying locusts
in the wake of wind whipped carrion.
The ruinous moth begrimed with filth
beckons the dread murk battalion.
Ashen wings purring in airy whispers
smothering the sighs of emptiness,
awakening the graves stinging embrace
and dank immortal nothingness.
I watch the amber night relume
as my shadow fades away.
The violet night has come hither
To join my farewell parade.

Beyond the End

Bards sing sad songs in the sunless brume
Reciting hushed liturgies in the funeral gloom.
My dimpling corpse upon a dour tear
The gnawing pyre beckons me near.
Ah! how long before my flesh flakes to soot?
And ash, I will become from head to foot.
Through Carmine flames of grief unrelenting
With raspy crackling of embers complimenting

The flicker and curls of the dancing blaze
That signal the penitent end of my days.
I can see the imperial turrets of heavens pearled gates
Where all we are supposed to be wryly resonates.
The weeping angels summoned me to atone
Before the lucent magisterial eternal throne.
And then the truths, as gaunt they be
Revealed themselves to set me free.
And I beheld the dazzling face of the Lord
Amongst the crumbling pavilions of an ethereal orb
And the skeleton of God fell limp and pale
Croaking his last like a rattle snakes tail.
The star of Bethlehem fell to earth
To burn in the sand with frankincense and mirth
And the moulted feathers of celestial swarms
Danced in the swirl of collapsing storms.
The illusion of the ether became the curse of the divine
And all I thought I knew had lost its shine.
Through the peevish gods wily deceit
With all who are born remaining incomplete
From guiltless infants to the verily condemned,
Even virgins turn into hags in the end.
A ghost I may be, a fugitive of naive futility.
On the wrong side of Heaven, to roam alone.... eternally .

Deathly times

I dreamt that I had died,
and was having tea with the dead..
in a dark deep place
eating a soft sponge of dread.
Everyone was smiling
but no one spoke.
I was about to say something
&.......then I awoke

From churchless lands

I look upon the resting place
of a far greater man than I,
of a great enchanter
under a bewitching cerulean sky.
Through paths of muffled primrose tufts
towards yonder grave a Druid sleeps,
where blue bells fill their cups with tears
and a great willow lazily weeps.
Crows fan their ink black wings
whilst leathery toads leap and croak,
timid hares dart left to right
between curious knots of Oak
laid to rest. Laid rest
In this magical pagan grove
bedewed with nectar and
the sourness of the sloes,
I rest my weary head
on the flowery lap of woe.
Could things have been any different?
Of that I shall never know.......

Is this how it ends.....

Knee deep in a river of tears
Wading through the fading years
The light of hope.. it disappears
Is this how it's meant to be?
I remember everything,
But who is left to remember me?
Sitting on a stranger's grave
Is this how it's meant to be?

Watching high the spin of the coin
Falling Heads & we grow old
Falling Tales & we die young
Is this how it's meant to be?
On the roll of the loaded dice
With the spin of the broken wheel
Your number's up and so are we
Is this how it's meant to be?
Under a winter white sky
Memories come and go
I remember who I was
But that was a lifetime ago.

The night's dominion

Death wrenching life from mothers clenching babes sleeping
Time dispensing oblivions impending despair ....unweeping
We look into the gorgon's eye unflinching
Into the lengthening shades of descending night unrepenting
Enwrapped in the nights sparkless dominion.
To wander its long bankless streams of mist
On bloodless drifting shrouds
That unwind into the unseen abyss
Death is but a path that must be trod
To lay alone in a darkly box
With splintery clusters of pine and clod
To sleep with worms and slowly rot

Yonder Lamps

We gaze at yonder Starry Lamps
Besprinkled in the night's hollow face,
We chase the dawn under the frown of dusk
To a place beyond hopes embrace.
In Death's infinite sleep
Where all sorrows are made,
Alongside the gold-eyed toad
We share the croaks of the grave.
We envy not the warmer clime,
That sears under a solar orbs glow
Inclined as we are to repose
As murk shades deep, deep below.

You Will Find Me at the Bottom of Your Grave

You will find me at the bottom of your grave,
Choking on dust and chewing on clay.
There is no need to get up,
You have a debt to death to pay.
Come hither the swarm of last breaths
Fluttering wheezes of sightless gasps,
Hovering above the impalpable hiss of Hades
To ebb into the aeons of the past.
Without love the world grows dim
It becomes blurred with broken hearts,
With each piece beating still
In the deep recesses of the dark.

Seeds so drear to swallow,

I have reaped the life that I have sown,
seeds so drear to swallow,
and now I walk this path alone,
where only death can follow.
Relentlessly woven is the weft
until the path is riven & cleft,
as the sun sets on my last breath
so life ends and born is death.
Robed in ruins sallow hue
among the cult of suffering rue.
To walk asunder nighted malign
'til the edge of churlish endless time.
The stars of night bathe in my tears
where eerie serpents lurk unseen,
To crawl across the timeless ash
under desolations drooping wings.
Through misery woods of spectral mist
where wolves howl and vipers hiss,
to fade beyond the realm of graves
in the dusk of all our yesterdays.
I have reaped the life that I have sown,
seeds so drear to swallow,
and now I walk this path alone,
where only death can follow.

A Cemetery Muse

The graves I see, like scattered seeds
never to bud, nor grow and break free
from the shy veil of stillness,
a gloom-swathed chillness
of sunken crooked stones
and flaking pine and bone.
Darkling shades bathe
in the still of dusk,
coddled in clod
and coffin handle rust.
The morning mist
bedewed with teary cries,
like shimmering ghosts
sodden in weary sighs,
but all I can see are
these marble slouching shrines
like empty hour glasses
broken on the brim of time.

A Deathly Visage

In the damp abiding realm
Of disquieting earthly woe
Clad in soil and turf
Where seeds can never grow,
We become frozen.
Like cold marble, lifeless,
With no heart to warm
The pearly stone likeness
Of who we once were;
Of what we could never become
With the threads of our lives
Once spun, and now undone.

It's Not So Lonely

There are many visitors
To keep me company as I lay.
It's surreal here looking up
At the knees of them and they
Who lay pretty flowers
Mumbling this and that,
Wishing I was alive,
But soon they will forget.
I have no idea
What's to become of my soul?
But it could be worse,
I could be alive in this hole.
The pigeons flap about
Above my shallow grave,
Ants scurry across me
Under the coffin lid shade.
Moles pass by occasionally
Worms drop in literally,
There's always something to do
Like plucking the roots of lilies.
It's a basic accommodation
There's no TV or comfy bed,
No warm pyjama's
Just a quilted pillow for my head.
You get used to the dark
The silence and the cold,
What you don't get used to
Is that your life's always on hold.
It's not too bad being dead,
A coffin can be quite homely.
And with all my passing guests,
It's not so lonely.

To Sup By Oblivions Shore

The necessity of death
Is the binding contract of birth.
It is assured as it is unalterable
And for what it's worth,
An irresistible conclusion
To what we never asked to be,
But here we are
Walking life's baffling journey;
And the bondsman of your heart
Shall break your terrestrial chains
And rob you of your dreams
As the blood leaves your veins.

We abdicate our moment in life
For an everlasting yawn,
Inside hollow blank dreams
That prophesise and forewarn.
In the grim hours of grief
There can be no forgiveness,
No forthcoming relief
From the coming sombre stillness.
One can ridicule decay
Mock passing's deathless repose,
But one cannot elude decay
Nor hide from collapsing shadows.

We become trembling unfettered shades
With terror fraught, and quaking woe
Like moths a fluttering on a starless night
With dusty wings afire below,

Insects sequestered from life
To be fading echoes in the unlit sky

That fade to faint murmurs
As ruthless time goes by.

A cup of bitter grief
A mug of sour woe
A bowl of Lethean despair
Mixed with cold sorrow;
To sup by oblivions shore
Upon a bank of dust and nettle,
By an ebbing tide of tears
We are a grain upon a speckle
In an ocean of loveless dust.
Befringed with deaths fruitless sting
Ah.. I must impart..
Weeping is a brittle feverish thing.

CHAPTER 6 - SONNETS

Impearled Tears

I walk with a rankling grief in my wake
My pain manifests in distant echoes
My heart is a cleft of loves rent arrows
Sometimes I feel my birth was a mistake.
With love, the emotion I must forsake
I am withering in the dim fallows ?
A fish gasping for air in the shallows?

Am I the fly in the web of times travail?
Where silken twines hook each artery beat?
Why does this dry bitter cup of sadness
Taste so sour yet ambrosial and sweet?
So I walk on a rice paper façade
With choking solitude below my feet
To the cavernous wheezes of blackness.

A Drear Sonnet

I wandered into the grim hours of woe
Into a chamber brimming with solitude
Where pendulous tears of icy grief accrued
That wept in the cold shaded darks hollow
Though nothing I witnessed, or could know
would make me understand, nor conclude
How my present plight could be viewed
as a living mirage of my shadow?

But here I was, in my unfeeling tomb
To wither in the sour stillness and cold
I was not a beggar, nor am I king
Thus in my pale form, I am to assume
If kindness was covetable as Gold
what ingots of joy would such passing bring.

In Life

In life we fall through the hurrying hours,
we dream, we laugh, we lament and we scream,
We hope, we love, we plot, and we scheme
We see red, we see yellow, green and blue
We survey in life, every type of hue,
We listen, learn, we hear the trees and birds
We find comfort with song and kindly words.

In life we feel and touch, we taste, and smell
And then it ends, bright colours fade away
We study the world through heaven and hell
No more to feel, nor see the bright of day.
Nothing left to hear except the cruel swell
Of the drowning dreams of life's slow decay.

ABOUT THE AUTHOR

Crin Hawk is vocalist of UK experimental black metal band, The Meads of Asphodel, and pagan metal band, The Wolves of Avalon [under the name Metatron] and founder of Godreah Records. Those know his lyrical muse; will be familiar with the dark side of human nature explored here.

This book of poetry is inspired by many emotions and events that have shaped his life. The love of his parents, wives, and relationships, with the ultimate demise of them all.

That in itself creates many of the feelings we all embrace or try to avoid [without success] at some point.

With his lyrical insight to the Meads of Asphodel album, The Murder of Jesus the Jew, his agnostic approach to religion reaches its scathing conclusion here.

The approach to the album, Sonderkommando [about the Holocaust], sent him on journey to Auschwitz, where a deep humbling before a fathomless grief inspired the said lyrics and many of the dark poetry herein.

The poetry also lays bare his cynical view of life, people and empathy for nature.

Metatron has previously stated,

"I cannot agree with the creator theory for why we are upon this Earth. Why create such a cruel world? To get a grasp of this statement we must review it again with Humanity taken out of the equation. Now look upon the world of nature and of a Creator who has designed its complex intricacies. There is still the yelping of creatures being eaten alive. There is still the blood thirst of the hunter and the cowering affright of the prey.

So an all seeing, all knowing Creator has still fashioned a world of pain, where the strong survive. It seems no different whether humans are part of this scheme or not. The blood spilling and primal need to survive remains the same. A conscience based being has no influence on this fact. If you can align yourself with such a Creator who would deliberately conceive a place where beings can rip each other to pieces [remember, we cannot blame humans as they hypothetically do not exist] then you must ask yourself why?"

ACKNOWLEDGEMENTS

Cover art by Crin Hawk
Cover art design by Rijkje Hawkes
Cover formatted by Jack Cowley
Book and eBook formatting by Ravi RamGati
Proofed by Karen Mills
Web page – Steve Thomas-Green

With deep gratitude
To my Mother and Father, who made me.
To my Sons and Daughter, who keep me old.
To my Grandchildren, who keep me young.
To the women who keep me mystified.
To the bands who keep me sane.
To the fans who make it all clear.
Byron Roberts [Bal Sagoth] for the exquisite Foreword

Metatron has written a lengthy treatise on the life of Jesus the Jew, with an insight to the historical figure of a man made God by his contemporaries.

Another treatise concerns the Holocaust, for which he was interviewed by the London Jewish chronicle for his lyrical interpretations of this prime example of man's inhumanity.

Both can be found on the Godreah web page as a separate codex.

For more information visit
www.godreah.com
email Godreah@ntlworld.com

Printed in Great Britain
by Amazon

63559996R00098